**Dangerous
Pursuit
of Yellow**

Dangerous Pursuit of Yellow

Annie Wright

Smokestack Books
1 Lake Terrace, Grewelthorpe, Ripon HG4 3BU
e-mail: info@smokestack-books.co.uk
www.smokestack-books.co.uk

Text copyright 2019,
Annie Wright,
all rights reserved.

Cover image:
Dana Schutz,
Lion Eating Its Tamer 2015,
courtesy of the artist
and Petzel, New York.

ISBN 9781999674236

Smokestack Books
is represented
by Inpress Ltd

*for my son Jacob
and in loving memory of
my brother in law Jim*

Contents

Dangerous Pursuit of Yellow	9
Indian Yellow	13
The Wounded Deer	15
Aycliffe Angels	16
Nine More Ways of Seeing	25
Ochre	29
Sussex Summers	31
The Jug My Mother Gave Me	32
Clearing Out	33
Relapse	34
Locked In	35
Erosion	36
Saffron	39
Ikegami	40
November Snowfall	41
Boogie Woogie, Goldhurst Terrace	42
Greer	44
Gamboge Genuine	47
Fairy Tale for a Hard Man	49
Winter Solstice on Redcar Sands	52
how the point was reached	54
After consuming three hundred lychees	55
Orpiment	59
Dulce Cor	61
His Lady, the Sparrow	62
Goldcrest	63
Prayers after La Prière	64
Deeply Sorry Atonement Poem	66

Cadmium Yellow	69
Devon April	71
After Apple Picking	72
Jimmy Wright	73
Frost	75
The House Where I Lived	76
rosy-fingered dawn at louse point	77
Domain Field	79

Dangerous Pursuit of Yellow

If you had known that prolonged use of absinthe might have caused, rather than exacerbated the epilepsy, and the thujone it contains could have manifested jaundiced visions; that the manias and exhaustion which triggered the depressions would lead you to drink turpentine, try to ingest the paint, which in turn provoked the hostility your friends fled from and the nausea and stomach aches which sent you staggering into fields under the fiercest suns; that the resulting sunstroke when you were consumed by suns, light, flowers, aggravated all your symptoms, had you devouring the paint chips, sending to Paris, London, for more tubes of lemon chrome, addicted to its vibrancy, outrageous hue, so the doctor had to treat you with digitalis to control the passions, seizures, the fits of gloom, thereby causing you to see only stil-de-grain and sulphurous spots, the poisoning from digesting lead chromate swelling your retinas so you hallucinated light in zinc white circles round the stars: would you have chosen another path, of sobriety perhaps, a modest life, instead of what's led to this pine box, haloed by last canvases, blazing rings of sunflowers and corn marigolds, and to those final words, tolling now for absent bells – *la tristesse durera toujours?*

Indian Yellow

Indian Yellow

Piss artists of Monghyr, my sisters
and I, we piss into history

chained to iron posts; men wrench
our mouths wide, force jaws

to chew mango leaves, pour pails
of muddy water down our throats.

We shit and piss our bedding,
trample the sodden straw

and every where the yellow stench
ulcerates our tongues.

Our swollen stomachs mock us;
we cannot stave off the pain.

We mourn the passing
of our starving young,

their jaundiced eyes and moaning,
praying Lord Krishna take notice.

When at last inspectors came
in their white helmets, fawn suits,

setting up camp under taut canvas,
all they saw was rivers of sunlight

washing over our legs, splashing
our hooves, a turmeric flood.

Cattlemen crated the drying heaps,
drove up the rupees for *purée of India*.

Krishna, if your dhoti were blue as
your skin and not canary yellow

would they beat us to chew hibiscus
or indigo, would they force fistfuls

of blazing sky down our throats?
Why won't you hear us crying?

There are no bells, no divine flute
only this stinking yellow fading

The Wounded Deer

after Frida Kahlo

In the forest of despair
I stumbled on naked truth
the cruelty of intimacy

betrayed – I am the hunted
tormented with arrows
that hit the mark over and over

the hounding of my soul
a ritual blood-letting
that maims before it kills

I cannot see myself – all
the mirror-pools are shrouded
am I not beautiful

as a youth? I have cut off
my braids, shrugging off
my woman's hide. Their dogs

will rip the vulnerable heart
from its mooring. It will bleed
fury and self-loathing

cuckold antlers mock me
baying dogs close in
I do not run but stand.

Aycliffe Angels

*'Those little angels of Aycliffe won't get away with it –
the Luftwaffe will bomb you out of existence.'*
Lord Haw Haw

I   The Shifting House

The drill: strip off, don thick white overalls,
check for contraband – cigarettes and lighters,
matches, jewellery, powder, lipsticks – anything

that might cause a spark. Only married lasses
could keep their wedding ring, taped over
withsticking plaster. We looked a sight, nothing

to write home about, in makeshift, knotted
turbans – hairclips not allowed – slathering
barrier cream into hairlines, faces, hands.

In the lines to cross over to the Clean Side
a sudden hush, as if we'd heard a pin drop.

II On The Clean Side

When I was told I'd been recruited for Filling
I thought *that's nice*; it sounded better than Explosives.

I wrote my mam that I'd been put on filling shells.
She was pleased, saying I'd always had light hands

for cakes and pastry. I didn't let on, found lodgings
in Darlington. I was assigned to workplace 29

in Sector 7A. When I walked in, the whole place smelt
sweet, like York in the rain, only it was cordite

being prepared for bullets. On first shift each week
the Blue Band read the rules. *No Talking* –

you could hardly hear above the drill of the machines
but it was bleak as prison, working in silence.

We packed shells with fulminate of mercury, sodium
thiosulphate, lead azide and placed the detonators.

You'd to keep your workbench spotless. *Strong Discipline,
Absolute Routine, Precision. No. Margin. For. Error!*

I learned slogans – *A Concealed Mistake Is A Crime.*
Total concentration is the best way of killing time.

III   The Fundamental Things Apply

In February 1942 we'd been on earlies
so Audrey and me arranged to meet one Friday
for High Tea and the pictures.

When it was our turn in the queue
a chap behind us started whistling
and his pal called out, *Well blow me,*

if it isn't a pair of Aycliffe canaries!
We went beetroot, under yellow stains
that all our scrubbing couldn't hide.

Audrey dug her hands deep into her pockets.
You pay, she whispered and I did
because my fingers were only a little brown.

We were all right in the dark
with Humphrey Bogart and Ingrid Bergman.
I wanted her to leave Laszlo, return to Paris

with him, even though you knew she couldn't.
When Rick put her on the plane with Laszlo
not himself, I sobbed and couldn't stop.

Next morning I could hear *A kiss is still a kiss*
as the Blue Band asked us to stand. I knew immediately.
There'd been an accident on lates –

two hundred pounds of fulminate exploded.
Edna, Irene, Alice and Phoebe gone,
instantly. We'd a minute's silence.

IV   Mad as Hatters

We needed cheering up that Spring
tramping in through unseasonal snow,
pathways sludged to mucky brown, so
when rumour of a visit to beat the King's

goes round, we're gathering snow in May,
buckets and shovels to the fields, in a rush
to lay a white carpet on top of the slush
for Churchill visits the Angels today.

Gladys Stoddart, demurest by far,
is chosen to greet him. We're in the line-up
praying Winnie's been warned not to light up
as she gives him a kiss – and a whopping cigar!

V The Mixing Shop

Jean volunteered for Sector One – I was never
brave enough, the 'suicide group' their nickname.

On second shift they heard a blast. White faces
peered out, saw a carrier girl stumbling blindly

on the dirty side. Propped against the shop door
lay the mixer lass, her hand blown off,

the white magazine suit ripped open, her body
torn and bleeding. The foreman caught

her last words, *Oh my poor bairn, my poor bairn.*

VI Waving the Flag

Doris had to escort the detonators
to be tested. She'd to walk slowly
waving a red flag, thirty yards
in front of chaps wheelbarrowing

the batches. Workmen repairing
the roadway thought it a huge joke
leaning out and resting on their picks
calling out all kinds of daftness

never knowing just one spark
could have blown them all sky high.

VII   The Lighter Side

We'd knock off, clatter up to Heighington
and let our hair down on the journey home.

I remember one young lad, green as willow,
got in our carriage after his first day.

Well, we'd high jinks, bumping into him
and jostling him into the middle.

Then Hannah Dixon calls out, *Eeh pet,
does your mammy know you'se out?*

We shrieked, his little face was scarlet
and someone starts up singing, *Mammy, mammy,*

how I love you, how I love you. We join in
singing and blowing pouty kisses. A big lass

plants a lipstick smacker, gets him in a dancing
hold, then grabs him by the belt and yells,

*Come on Johnny, give the girls a treat, show us
your maiden's prayer! At him lasses!*

We all pile on, wrestle him down and grab
his legs. Someone gets his shoes off,

a tussle for his trousers and they're hoyed around.
That's enough ladies, keep the poor lad decent!

It was Olive Moreland rescued him, but not before
his trousers had been hung out the carriage window.

VIII The Final Blow

News of Hitler's death came over on the wireless
and made the morning papers. Like wildfire spreading,

everyone was saying it couldn't be much longer,
daring to believe it really was the end, so whether

someone was lax we never knew, but the worst
blast of all happened that morning of May 2nd –

they heard the explosion in Darlington. We lost
Alice Wilson, William Mitchell, both single,

James Brunton, Isabella Bailey, William Hobson,
Christopher Seagrave and Edmund Smith, all

married, and Elsie Barrett, widow. The cruellest
blow; six more days and they'd have made it safe.

IX   Now the Blinking War is Over

When it ended I was very sad.
We had our photos taken, section by section
No more ROF for me

Once we'd partied for VE day and toasted
lost friends, it was tidy up, wait for decommission
You can tell the blinking Blue Band
Where to shove the blinking pass

Nine More Ways of Seeing

for Gordon Hodgeon

I
black and gold minstrel
crooning to Billy Cotton's
band, tail feathers high

II
blackbird summons pluck
battling against Nor' Easters:
sleet and ice, mud, fog

III
blackbird ruffles some
feathers careering around
Cleveland's sea-worn hills

IV
Potto whips Loftus
At Marton crossroads waiting
for God or Eston

and Pallister: bleak
bird – killing time astride
old Skinningrove's works

V
backbone of iron
and steel worn out – last chorus
for the blasting men

unloading ore at
Teesport, titanium's the future,
bird divines

VI
eloquent blackbird
even a cage with stout bars
can't suppress the song

VII
winter breaks: blackbird
flies past the fairy lights of
ICI Wilton

VIII
in a remote world
feathers become seams of jet
bird takes up the quill

IX
blackbird in lilac
blossom: something salvaged from
the cruel month's end

Ochre

Ochre

ancient of crones
witness to Time

arrows tipped
with my bones

mud and stone
river   rock
       washing continents
             flooding   plains

I am
squabble of goose
hunger of bear

            fire and earth
            stick   clay
            not   dancer
                but flame

mud and bone
      river   rock
      drenched by oceans
           rinsing sand

                    ogra ogra
                    desert   rays

                    ocrum ocrum
                    chant   drum

                    yellow spot
                    becomes sun

I am
desert amber
maize cob   leaf fall

woodsmoke   deer fat

                        fire and earth
                        stick   flint
                        not   painter
                                 but   skin

                        fire and earth
                        pelt   cave
                        not   warrior
                                           but   grave

when rock become river
sea become fire

at Earth melt and Time end
when history expire

as the kiln cool
and clay meld with bone

my sandy thumbprint
last mark on stone

Sussex Summers

Bracklesham Bay, East or West Wittering,
ramshackle bungalows, other folks' games,
Junior Scrabble, beachcombing sunsets, breezes

tattering unruly hair. Unwieldy deckchairs, gutsy breezes
upskittling blankets and picnic box, mum wittering
on about sand in the lunch. Ritual games

burying dad, digging sand boats, seawater moats, game
of changing without showing bare bottoms, the breeze's
twitch and slap of towels, swallows on the wires twittering

much wittering re trains back to Fetcham, last game,
    summer's breezy salute

The Jug My Mother Gave Me

was kept under the sink. An old crazed jug
she used sometimes for sweet peas or roses.
I liked how it bellied out, skimming in
to a high waist and curving out, the shape

of a woman, handle a bent arm on hip.
A survivor, floating up from the waves
of all our house moves unremarked, intact.
And sometimes I would delve for it

preferring it to her crystal vases.
After the wreckage of my marriage
she had a box of bits out, sorted
for chucking. *You might want this –*

it belonged to Nana. Its ridged coils
are ripples on water. I run my fingers
over the bumpy surface. *A cheap thing
that took her eye on a seaside trip.*

This pot was thrown, made by a potter
whose indigo mark is clear on the base.
Its glaze shifts from aqua green to deeper
turquoise and blotchy bladderwrack brown.

The glaze is lustrous; where the sun strikes
it gleams like mother of pearl. Nana would burst
into the kitchen, in tight-waisted coat and hat.
God love those little bairns! she'd say, handing

hatpin, hat and coat over, then arms outstretched
to pick us up for cuddles. Baby back in her chair,
she'd bounce me on her lap as mum brewed tea.
Down at the bottom of the deep blue sea

I giggle and squirm as she drops me
into the net of her skirt and hoists me back
catching little fishes for my tea.

Clearing Out

after a line by Eavan Boland

Like oil lamps we put them out the back
along with bin bags full of clutter unfit
for charity. Mantles, once bright, disintegrate
to dust. Rusted winders refuse to budge.
Oiling with kindness might exercise
some stiffened parts, but seems futile
when the spare wicks are long since lost.

We kid ourselves the new home – that costs
an arm and a leg – with its sincere file
of thanks from relatives of those who've died,
is as caring as they come. How can I judge?
Cogs of her rusty mind ratchet oddly. I interrogate
staff about hair, nails, diet to flit away the guilt;
as if any of this could give her what she lacks.

Relapse

It is there, hanging in the shadows
under his eyes when, after broken nights, he rouses

himself for work; there in the shortness of breath
he's never suffered from before; there in the sudden
loss of weight. We thought he'd seen the death

of those growths in his neck which now appear
larger. He, who's always loved his bike, can only cycle
short distances. No-one's saying much to him for fear

of opening what cannot be contained. He's back on
the strict diet and all the alternative therapies, which,
we need to believe, will work again. When he's gone

to the doctor there must come time for the word
no-one utters, but everyone's heard.

Locked In

for Gordon

*Et la lune descend sur le temple qui fût
(Images 1907, Debussy)*

And the moon goes down over the temple that was
And the temple that was struggles for breath
And struggles for breath punctuate the rhythm of the voice
And the voice remembers from far off the owl's haunting cry
And the haunting cry is what he remembers of lost time
And time lost sighs, being breathed into the locked room
And the locked room despairs that the only key has flown

Erosion

i.m. Jim Ostler

Tides crash against cliffs, force air in cracks
so pressure builds as waves hurl sediment
until stuffed air explodes and rocks fragment.
Dwellings and coastal paths on edge roll back,
retreating further inland year by year.
The Holbeck Hall Hotel and Kettleness
toppled like skittles – while Holderness
dissolves under a barrage of salt. We fear

grief's erosion, how it will wear away
defences, seize memories from us, year
by crumbling year. Our last trip was to drive
beyond Caernarfon: wet October day,
the silted mud flats full of wading birds,
gulls and oystercatchers' plaintive cries.

That skirl of lament recalls you playing Irish pipes,
your strong, erratic voice – unbeached, alive.

Saffron

Saffron

Insubstantial as an aura, I am the begetter
of miracles. My devotees keep watch for the one day
when fields become seas of purple silk.

From rosy dawn women heap their baskets
with skirts of crocus, backs bent in supplication.
The honey scented air hangs languorous.

Flower mountains are tipped on trestle tables.
All afternoon they pluck red stigmas, discard
the petals. Peasant hands bear my stigmata.

Thousands of crimson fibres like spun sugar
lie in china bowls. This is my harvest gift,
its price far beyond rubies or gold.

Tonight men will bag the harvest; women
dizzy with scent will go home light-headed.
I will make them laugh, all aches forgotten.

After sunlit rice they will tease their men,
coppery fingers unbuttoning shirts, shedding skirts
for their fiery couplings under the fizzing stars.

Whilst they sweat and grunt abandoned
I will weep. I ease their menstrual cramps,
their bloody labours, yet I am barren.

Beware my bitter curse: blood-orange nightmare,
aromatic ruin. Wars have been fought and lost
in my name. This year I might manifest

or not, ruby purple bleeding into apricot and gold.
I will bankrupt your days, desiccate your nights,
dye the winding sheet, dance with the funeral flames.

Ikegami

after paper flowers by Isabell Buenz

I offer you a paper flower
don't read anything into it

it's my clumsy attempt to say
when words fail gather the fallen

like petals, wrap round your fingers
bind with glue from dream-stitched eyes

think of this as a touch paper –
here, catch it

ignite

November Snowfall

Snow has tenderly covered us
overnight, slowing the A1 traffic

to an eerie pavane. In a long hour
I chug fewer than ten miles

down to barely moving. I daren't turn
the engine off, afraid it won't restart

tuned to each rattling cough, the girls
nebulise your airways clear

vehicles leave unaccustomed gaps
like conversations with your dearest friends

where silence is smiling and easy. Beyond
the windscreen is a virgin landscape

winter trees, dragon's breath, snow crusting
the peaks of your beloved mountains

I am gentled along, sliding, skidding
hours late for a difficult appointment

but there's no panic. Wreathed in steam
from my tea I watch ecstatic children

my sister tucks you in the softest blanket
places one of the girls' teddies by your hand

they need no lessons in how to use
this unexpected gift, live each moment

in snowballs, makeshift toboggans
snowmen rising like unwieldy dough

when you come home, you say, you want
to make her barabrith and marmalade

Boogie Woogie, Goldhurst Terrace

Ribbons of terraces unfurl
from Swiss Cottage down to Kilburn,
flats and bedsits – precariously stacked boxes,

weekend manic idleness winding
down. Two women park a wheelchair
heave a man indoors.

Night breath is cool. Jazzy stars
slink to the microphone, a flurry of leaves
turns amber under streetlights

pennies from heaven – Jenny's bruises
are healing, her ground floor door
is locked.

Someone's trying notes in two-tone –
black suit, white shirt, pork pie hat.
Cabbage and bratwurst drifts down.

In candlewick dressing gowns
emigré sisters clean their teeth
the mad one gargling snatches of Kurt Weill.

On such a night as this
someone believed he could fly
stepped from a bedroom window.

The women link hands
begin to lift him upstairs.
The younger sister's back with Bertolt

in Berlin, waiting on the landing,
in the wings, before the dramatic
exit into exile, whilst

fifteen doors down, a single lamp
burns in the surgery. Dr Goldscheider
sits alone, absorbed in his Kandinsky.

Carrying her toothbrush like a spear
the one who moans but never speaks
strides out from the bathroom

startling the women who lose their grip
and drop the man two stairs short
of safe landing. Her face creases

and she hoots, setting everyone off howling,
chortling as they clutch the banisters.
Reds, blues and yellows erupt

saxophone and trumpet virtuosos
flood the canvas, layering over
the persistent rumble of the Bakerloo.

Greer

after portrait by Paula Rego

It's the feet she wanted me to notice: the corns,
callouses and bunions – sturdy feet that dig
the onion patch, at ease with soil and worms,

feet that dwell in comfortable shoes – a man's loved
lace-ups, splitting at the seams, blacked and buffed
to a sheen, leather worn soft as familiar gloves.

My imaginary gran; the eccentric one
in sheer black tights, barely disguising hairy calves,
scarred and bony knees, the sort to keep exactly

the kind of bolt, screw or planks needed to fix
a go-cart, build a rocket from an eight year old's
design. Labourer's hands can swing you at speed

or mend your mother's leaking downpipe. She collects
dresses like an ageing queen, but don't be deceived.
See how the feet meet, sole to sole, how elbows flex

thighs like butterfly wings. This monarch
possesses the stamina to traverse continents. I see
blood-orange rootedness, the dress worn archly

as a Buddhist's robe, genderless. Under its folds
breasts flop unrestrained. For all the apparent anarchy,
there's dogged belligerence in this pose.

Age lines can't conceal vivacious eyes,
high cheekbones. A coquettish toss of the head, wild
hair betray the flirting with ideas. That roguish smile,

lips puckered to laugh as much at self as others,
proclaims *Hey guys – you know what? I'm not
finished yet* and that infamous cackle erupts.

Gamboge Genuine

Gamboge Genuine

Once you've discovered me you'll never touch
Cadmium, Bismuth or Nickel Titanium again.
Delicate Aureolin will fail to tease your palette.
Pursue me only if you are genuinely seeking
the exact tint of lemons, fresh, sharp as birdsong,
light-reflecting but not shining. I will wash
over you, faithfully portraying your pitted peel.
You will praise my degrees of density, still claim
you can see right through me. Poor fool.

You may not obtain me until I am ten years old;
it will cost you dear. The farmer will not tell you
how the fields are mined, how many suitors have lost
a hand, an arm, a leg. *Liaison c'est dangereuse, nest-ce pas?*
You are determined. Before the peasant be sure to praise
my twelve inch waist, my budding growth. Slant-eyed,
I will not look at you when I am chosen. Don't mumble
Morella, Hanburyii. Call me by my familiar names:
Gummi Gutta, Gom Guttae, Tom Rong, Gutta Gamba.

Bring cloth-wrapped coins, a bamboo pot,
your keenest knife. I beg one favour. Sharpen it
so the blade would glide through ox hide, sever
the windpipe at a stroke. On the day of possession
I will look steadfastly at you. Lift the knife,
invoke your gods – I will not tremble – but, I pray you,
slit me clean and swift. Tie your bamboo cup
below the cut to catch the milky yellow
as it bleeds from me. Proof of my honour.

Retreat. I will not have you see me weep.
Retreat, and if you escape the killing fields,
you may return with the rains next year to claim
your booty. You will slash the rope, wrench it
from my thickening waist, break the bamboo mould,
lift the rounded resin block up high and yell,
Dark saffron, murky orange, amber! To test
the contract, you will lick the surface of the gum.
Though you destroy me, I cannot play you false.

No taste on your tongue, then brilliantly acrid.
You will spit it, rinse your mouth out.
The second test, you sniff the no-smell
as saffron rays glint young leaves. If you could
hold a full dose in your mouth and swallow,
first it would cure you of your worm,
then kill you. This third test you decline.
You snatch your prize. I watch you go
to melt your money, see it pour in brassy rivers.

I wonder what it would feel like to lie naked
on a rattan bed, barely breathing, trembling,
for an artist. Would he praise my mustard skin,
dappled with light from the melting corncobs
of wisteria? Or work the brush in his mouth
to the finest point? Would the sable tip lift
translucent pigment, feather reflected highlights
in my olive eyes? Would his true art foresee what you
could not: the bullet intended for my own pure heart?

Note: Gamboge is still collected from Cambodia from areas rife with unexploded landmines. When melted down, a recent consignment for Winsor and Newton was found to contain 5 bullets.

Fairy Tale for a Hard Man

i.m. Jackie Leven

Who was born in poor toun
A wild and headstrong boy
A wandering vein thrummed in his blood
Summoned him into the void

He sought his education
Roaming Kirkcaldy's hills
First to be expelled from school
Pursuing illicit thrills

Romany boy beset by gangs
He ran away from Fife
As if he could escape his fate
He and his fresh young wife

> *Eternal is the warrior*
> *Who finds beauty in his wounds*
> Who dwells among the hard men
> Turns cruelty to haunting tunes

When Jackie climbed the dream stalk
He saw his only choice
To step inside the giant mind
And steal the golden voice

Hitching through Europe's cities
The dives and crazy pubs
He tuned his guitar to pain
Sang of violence and drugs

One bleak night in London town
Thugs tried to strangle him
Left for dead without his voice
He turned to heroin

> *Eternal is the warrior*
> *Who finds beauty in his wounds*
> Who thrown in the waters of despair
> Alone and bereft near drowns

When a princess came visiting
And begged him for a song
He gave *The Bonnie Earl of Moray*
His alto bruised but strong

A good woman stepped onto the path
With a voice to soothe his own
He made a vow, followed her south
Finally found a home

> *Eternal is the warrior*
> *Who finds beauty in his wounds*
> Who has survived the dark one's touch
> Under an ailing moon

Many's the tale that spiced the songs
That'd have you split your sides
Crying into a pint of ale
Until you thought you'd die

One day the giant began to fade
Cut back to mortal size
But few kenned what was happening
Before their very eyes

Mortally ill he lay dying
And smelt a sweet green wood
Hear a giant singing where
Jackie Leven once had stood

> Grieve for a man too early gone
> Follow his voice and swoon
> *Eternal is the warrior*
> *Who finds beauty in his wounds*

Winter Solstice on Redcar Sands

i.m. Vicki Thomas, founder Vane Woman and poet

I'd been looking out for
a murmuration
since September. Clacking,

jabbering, they swoop
and soar, North East birds
on a feisty jolly

your *darling bad starlings*
outchatter the surf.
Up the coast blast furnaces

billow steam again –
ironic twist of empire, Tata
and Sahaviriya the masters now.

Bolckow and Vaughan lie bemused
in their graves. Time like the tide
has toppled kings. But a villain

thought lost in mud re-emerged.
Through a forensic lens, evil
cripple transmutes to warrior-hero,

history remade, a *crown… on fire.*
You always knew this. On a knife-edge,
like Janus you could see both ways,

the uncomfortable edge of things.
We hunch against the wind, traipse
across drifting sands. All the way

to the car park I think of you,
and how today the earth will turn
inexorably towards the light.

What we can't know yet is how light
will tug, its magnetic shift summoning
you, too soon, into the brilliance.

how the point was reached

after Gillian Allnutt

where he could endure no longer and fell
and how they fell to, unloading cotton, mahogany
and how he was unloaded in an unmarked spot

and how Gillows' mahogany furniture made a name
and how the cotton tree grew tall and strange
and how fidelity unmarked was not forgotten

and how rains fell and storm years lashed
and how a stone was raised to his fidelity
and how human cargo lashed and bound ceased

and how we came seeking a name
and how children had painted *Samboo* on stones
and how we followed the causeway to the point

where beyond tides and storms his name endures

After consuming three hundred lychees

Su Dongpo is ready to compose a poem.
He unrolls paper across the floor,

takes up brush, ink, inkstone – the four
precious things – lifts brushfuls of water

onto stone. He grinds the ink in smooth
circles into the water. A black hole swirls

and thickens. Su Dongpo thinks of the moon,
of biting into the milky cheeks of concubines

and his long dead wife steps into the room.
The ink releases its particular fragrance –

autumn smoke from pine wood mingling
with soot, feathered from funnels

of lamps, deer horn boiled to rancid glue
overlaid with musk and crushed jade.

The moon has not yet risen. Shavings
of lychee shells, stippled pink, gleam

by hearthlight, littering the floor. Ebony beans
reflect the night. Su Dongpo's wrist flows

wanting to let a poem bubble out from a hole
in the clouds, cascade down the mountain

but the worthy subjects have left. His gut
is seized with dragons of fire in combat.

Almighty rumble. Ignoring the cloud-head brush,
he chooses the axe-head for cutting strokes

swings the brush and chops. Characters tumble
and stack up into *A Lament for Lychees*.

Orpiment

Orpiment

A candle to enter, sir. Set it down
away from your face. Ignore the growling,
the bark's worse than the bite; she will settle.

We're lucid today sir, quite transparent.
When your eyes accustom, you might see the shine;
there are days she can still take your breath away.

Delusions? And some! *King's Yellow* we call her
with her airs and graces. You name
the European court she hasn't dazzled in!

The only one fit for king's robes, angels' wings,
haloes and nimbuses, Egyptian sarcophagi, Doge's
robes; I could go on. Ah, I should tell you

we might lapse into Italian, old Italian,
or possibly Venetian. There's not a Tintoretto
Tiepolo or Titian we don't lay a claim to.

Watch how we introduce ourselves – there's a clue:
Konigsgelb, Rausch gelb, jaune Royal,
all better signs. Arzicon, auripigmentum,

be on your guard. *Oropimento*, warning bells,
Giallo Reale, Giallo del Re, we're volatile,
Giallo di Arsenico, make your farewells.

She's sensitive about her face so if you don't mind,
don't spark her off. We don't want her erupting.
Her skin's crumbling to powder; we daren't wash her.

Take this scented handkerchief. I'll warn you
the stench in there is rotten eggs and urine.
Terminal, of course. Can't be much longer now.

A miracle she's here at all. Arsenic, sir.
One hundredth of the dose she calls her *ratsbane*
would be enough to kill off you or me.

Did I mention not to let her touch you?
Well, if she does, don't put your fingers
anywhere near your mouth. You'll go through

cleansing when you emerge. Don't overtire her;
two or three minutes. We owe her that. For all our madness,
in our day sir, I think we must have been sublime.

No, I'll be right here. Find the door and I'll let you out.
You're quite safe here with us sir, safe as a gold vault,
safe as the grave. You can enter now.

Dulce Cor

When John Balliol died
she had his heart cut out

embalmed and cased
in ivory, dipped

and sealed in silver,
kept it always with her.

Lady and Abbess
benefactress of Balliol

designer of the first
stone to bridge the Nith,

she envisioned that
spannable gap.

When Devorgilla died
her monks had his heart

buried next to hers
enfolded in her arms –

the renamed abbey
her embalming.

His lady, the Sparrow

after Catullus, i.m. Mary Roberts

His lady, his little pet sparrow, is dead.
She who stayed by his side for nearly sixty years,
whom he loved more than his own eyes, is no more.
His honey, following him in place of her mother,
playful and teasing, her chirruping song for him alone.

Almost overnight her bodyweight plummeted
To featherlight bones, wren in a sparrow's frame.
She clung to the perch in the care home's cage
afraid to fly; wings fluttered, trembled, folded
and all her dunnocky browns dimmed.

Now she is beyond coaxing to peck at crumbs
or sip drops of water from a pipette, eyes filmed
over with grey veils. It is he whose eyes are weary
and red, whose solace must be the narrow bed
of ill tumours. Oh cold-hearted Venus, cruel Cupid,

mourn what you began in the drabness of war
and grieve for the lady, comfort the man.

Goldcrest

for David Underdown

Not a hurt hand,
he is cradling
a fledgling bird
willing it to live.

It must have hit glass,
eyes two Os of surprise,
beak a slender point
of the finest pencil.

The lines it might
have drawn, curves,
loops and swoops -
not this full stop.

Tinier than a wren
he says *scarcely seen*.
The flash on its brow
is school bus yellow.

A puff of sifted flour
he gentles into my palm;
down fluffing stirs
in a lift of air

as if

Prayers after La Prière

Man Ray 1930

1

Afterwards she finds herself praying,
hoping she's got away with it.
Life briefly carries on, as though
she's still the apple of his eye.

It isn't anger that alerts her
but the reluctance of the footsteps.
Abasing herself before the judgement
she attempts to conceal cunt and anus,

fingers copying the fig's broad leaves
so when she's found out, what He sees
is not woman, but a fallen apple,
cheek blemished by a bruising shadow.

Between them snakes a line in the earth
she can never re-cross.

2

She takes the only chair. When they enter
the cubicle, sit together on the low bed,
looking up with synchronised concern,
she knows at once.

Days later and still dazed,
letters are flying between hospitals,
copied to her. She's reduced to *rectum,
anal, anus; cell types adeno, squamous.*

Nor does *Female, 58, Patient,* adequately fit.
Extremely rare, early, fluid, another opinion,
has her google for knowledge on the Apple
to protect her rectum, her anus from radical

excision. A line's been crossed:
she finds herself praying to a greater god.

Deeply Sorry Atonement Poem

to Pete Mortimer for missing a poetry reading; after Glyn Maxwell

I am sorry, very sorry, the sorriest of all,
far sorrier than Heather when she split up with Sir Paul,
more sorry than the French when Rome invaded Gaul,
more penitent than Peter when he heard the cock's third call.

I'm more miserable than Carragher when he missed that penalty kick,
more shame-faced than Sven Eriksson when outed by Ulrik
ah! – I've more humiliation than a contestant on Big Brother
when all the votes to dump him have been backed up by his mother.

I've the contrition of the chap who fell at the Fitzwilliam,
broke three priceless vases and then found out they'd bill him;
I'm more apologetic than the gent who shot his beater
or Prescott when the press revealed he was a cheater.

So I'm deeply, humbly sorry to the Editors at Iron –
and it's true the bed you make you have to lie on –
I've spent the last few weeks slumped over in 'own goal' fits
for being in Kirkby Stephen when I should have been at Colpitts.

Cadmium Yellow

Cadmium Yellow

after Dana Schutz

You dare harangue me about pollution!
You're the ones who've poisoned all the seas
and land by tipping clapped-out batteries

in toxic dumps. Those Euro politricksters
should clean up their own messes
before they pontificate over mine.

Health and safety cuts no ice here;
artists have been wearing gloves for years
before they handle my bodily fluids.

King of the cadmium pride, that's me,
in my New York taxi coloured pelt,
not some circus beastie in a Big Top show.

The more they dilute me, the stronger
and fiercer I fight back; my ingenuity
indomitable as my staying power.

First I spread a rumour of scarcity.
No need to fan the flames of panic, simply
lie back and relish fevered speculation.

Suddenly trade in me is roaring;
artists, conservationists, they're all
stockpiling – I'm more in vogue than ever

so when Brussels bureaucrats pronounce
a full-on cadmium veto, they play
right into my paws. I hire a marquee

as pop-up gallery, invite the whole circus
to ringside seats. Lights dim, drums roll,
the tamer ushers me into the ring.

I take my place on an upturned barrel
but there's no jumping blazing hoops.
Before I'm banished I've a vanishing

trick of my own to perfect. The canvas floor
islaid for dinner. I tuck a napkin under my chin,
twirl an ivory fork, open my jaw in an indolent yawn.

Down the jugular slips tamer and canvas
after brilliant canvas – Monets, Matisses,
Warhols, Koons and Picassos. The crowd gasps

at a world several hundred shades
greyer. I lick my chops. Now for dessert.
I'm loving this so much I could eat

myself. First down the hatch goes tail
and hindquarters, followed by fore limbs
and torso. Head and sunset mane

disappear into a black hole. Silence.
I watch their faces blench and no-one
moving. Houdini-like, I give it two full minutes –

before I re-emerge, blindingly
into the light, regurgitating paintings
in all their dazzling glory. A few months

is all it takes for Brussels to relent,
but be warned my friends; next time
it'll be for real and no coming back.

Devon April

I climbed a little hill to get a signal –
you've never understood how mobiles work.

Think of it as long-distance semaphore,
My sister beaming messages in red and yellow

flags. *Much better, sitting up and smiling,
nurse trying to give the diuretic orally.*

Mum, I picked wild flowers for you
as I did sixteen Aprils ago after dad died.

Everything in the hedgerows is vibrant yellow,
glossy celandines, petals splayed in sun salutes,

shaggy dandelions, the countrywoman's diuretic,
willow catkins turned to pollen-tipped feather dusters.

Gorse runs rampant as it did through childhood.
I fold a dock leaf to pick two sprigs; its scent

of coconut enticing early bees. Primroses spread
their petticoats in a very un-prim-like way.

White stitchwort quilts the verges, as neat
on the under-side as the front, immaculate

as your own stitchwork. At the end of the lane
a single Devon violet. The flowers you picked

as a child for your mother and she wept,
violets being the last gift of your sister Joan

who died of meningitis, aged five. You at ninety one
hang on, not ready yet to let your petals fall.

After Apple Picking

All is quiet again in the convent garden
except for wasps lurching in and out
of boozy holes. For the past hours

we have picked Bramleys, Cox's Orange
Pippins, Lord Lambournes and Pink Ladies.
The children armed with fishing nets

received the catch, laid it apple by apple
into the boxes. Sister Francis set us
going, the other sisters slipping in and out

to watch, almost unnoticed. An hour in
we stopped for photos and to try one,
the children opting for Pink Ladies

excited by their teeth marks bleeding red.
Grown-ups chose Lord Lambournes,
exquisite mix of sharp, sweet and juice,

never before tasting this alive. Soon the last
four sisters in their brown habits must leave,
too old, too few; the convent will be sold

and there'll be no more Carmelites here, tending
walled gardens, going about their quiet work,
fading like the Poor Clares, or forgotten apples.

Jimmy Wright

Your pocket watch, silver and precise, a driver's
metronome for knowing when to stoke,
to ease off, you made your trains run on time, chugging
or flying down the East Coast line.

LNER man to the core, you loved Worsdell locomotives,
your Darlington G5 256, kept the cab immaculate
with gleaming brass, swigged sweet black tea
from pop bottles, heated on the fireman's shovel.

Your sons brushed your boots with Cherry Blossom
one apiece, racing to outshine each other;
the reward to ride the footplates with you, feed
the firebox, toot the whistle, turn the valve.

Once you drove the royal train; on arrival
lined the crew up for the handshake.
Each tipped according to his rank –
for you a sovereign, never spent.

Approaching a station you'd toss a penny
down the platform, gauge its fall and stop
so the cab lined up precisely with the coin.
If you lost (you never did),

your sons could keep the copper.
Conscientious objector, was it a reserved
occupation kept you safe in the Great War?
I wear the white poppy in your name,

have always loved the massive, iron beasts
addicted to that male smell of coal, oil, steam,
huffing and chuffing from another age.
Dead before I was born, you remained remote

until one Saturday evening, driving to Whitby,
on a whim we took the Eskdale road. At Grosmont
Crossing a steam train fired up, ready to depart.
We leaped out. The new Tornado, Pacific,

typeA1 in green and gold and polished brass, showed off
its Darlington plate. I watched its perfect clouds puff
and fall, saw you in uniform beaming at me, froths
of steam drifting over us like cherry blossom.

Frost

Telling my son of mornings I used to wake and ice
had invaded in the night, seizing the insides
of bedroom windows, hanging its dinosaur incisors
from the guttering, Jacob is dubious. This child
of the new century, of central heating, global warming,
can't appreciate the barbarian beauty of frost.

It's the Iceni tribe, pitted against the might
of Rome, winning by stealth. Spears and daggers
festoon the glass, or bizarre leaf patterns.
Chilblains forgotten, I'm tiptoe on the lino,
tracing over the designs, trying to memorise
each fantastic pane.

Down in the cutting
dragon's breath from the steaming monster
is frozen in mid-air, held in a vice.
On the walk to school
we'd hunt for frozen puddles, to be the first
to crack the glaze.

Boys made long slides across the playground,
challenged girls to skid,
but I was mesmerised by the crates of milk,
glass columns pushed up from the bottles,
bluetits pinching cream from under
the silver caps.

When Mr Jones rang the bell
we settled to arithmetic, spelling
and watching the billy goat butt the wire fence
splintering icicles.

My son is unconvinced.
I freeze frame it all, before it's lost.

The House Where I Lived

The house with the flying freehold.
The house with an under dwelling we flooded.
The house with a cache of Jack's angry letters.
The house with a cast iron range.
The house with stone stairs mum tumbled down.
The house with no heating and no hot water
That snowed us in for weeks.
The house with a tree he fell from, wielding a chainsaw.
The house with stone mullions and Puritan roots.
The house with a twin tub ruining clothes
And a dark secret rose.
The house with a wooded garden and no central heating.
The house with walls two feet thick, steeped in dissent.
The house in league with Hollins wood
Where I would run to cry.
The house in the town four storeys high.
The house with toxic gas fires
That lured him onto the roof.
The house where I discovered tall stories.
The house with an attic darkroom
And all its stained glass intact.
The house with nowhere outside
From where I became a bride.
The house in the valley above the mill chimney
With water from Singing Brink.
The house with a cowboy spirit and toilet
Flushing hot water.
The house with the song of the River Colden
Rinsing her widow's weeds.
The house with sandblasted ceilings.
The house of millstone grit.
The house where I found my muse.
The house with the bridge where I dropped
Wishing pennies.
The house I walked out of to go to Sudan.

rosy-fingered dawn at louse point

after painting by Willem De Kooning

waking
at 4am
she saw
        he'd gone
                flit
                        in the night

no note
loose coins
tossed
on the bastard floor

running
        to the edge
                of the point

the dawn
lit
the peach
of her slip

fired rage
at a washed out
life

she hit
the deck

        relentless dawn
        brushed over
        jaundiced tears
        bile ranting

    cut
      a mean
          tango
              over the scene

yellowjack jerk
daubed over
      with hot
           sassy ingots
of pure
gold

Domain Field

Antony Gormley installation of 240 life-size forms in the Baltic

From the viewing platform the ground
below is empty, zero people in
the gallery, the end of day lull

matrices of people: winter trees
in a spare landscape, full
of the memory of fall

a solitary man weaves a path
through, glints of sun highlight
maybe shoulder, knee, hint of calf

we walk down metal stairs
enter the silvered chamber
the air tastes clearer

like after rain or showers.
A field of warrior spirits
begins to form. As we walk

between them the forms vibrate,
shimmying steel, matrix of neural
pathways, lit up, connecting –

even the particles of dust are
simmering. I find my self
can't stop tears brimming

when you peel back the skin
the flesh, lift out the bones
this is what is left

a spark of divinity
welded to essence
shimmering in the ether

if ash could be laid
on ash, spark-welded into
form, those other holy ghosts

might yet rise up
spirits unforgotten,
reclaiming ground.

Acknowledgements

Thanks are due to the editors of the following publications where some of these poems were first published: *The Black Light Engine Room, Diamond Twig, Ink, Sweat and Tears, Second Light, Tears in The Fence*; Andy Croft *et al* (eds) *How Things are Made: Poems for Gordon Hodgeon* (2009), S.J. Litherland *et al* (eds), *NORTHbound* (2016).

Ikegami was one of eight poems selected by Marjorie Lotfi Gill, poet in residence at Dumfries and Galloway's Spring Fling 2015. Artist Sue Stewart responded by designing the poems as posters/art cards exhibited at the Wigtown Book Festival.

The 2 line refrain quoted in 'Fairy Tale for a Hard Man' is taken from a Jackie Leven song 'Main Travelled Roads '.

I am indebted to Victoria Finlay whose book *Colour: Travels through the Paintbox* (2002) first inspired me to begin writing about the yellow pigments.

My heartfelt thanks to poets Tamar Yoseloff, S.J. Litherland and Marilyn Longstaff, and to Vane Women for all the advice, encouragement and support.